IMAGES
of England

AROUND
ASCOT

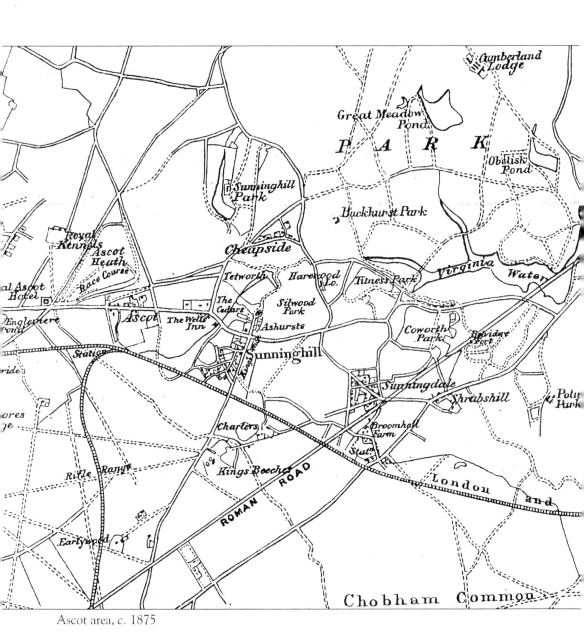

Ascot area, c. 1875

IMAGES
of England

AROUND
ASCOT

Compiled by
Reg Morris

TEMPUS

First published 1999
Copyright © Reg Morris, 1999

Tempus Publishing Limited
The Mill, Brimscombe Port,
Stroud, Gloucestershire, GL5 2QG

ISBN 0 7524 1573 5

Typesetting and origination by
Tempus Publishing Limited
Printed in Great Britain by
Midway Clark Printing, Wiltshire

Acknowledgements

First and foremost I would like to thank all the photographers who captured these moments in time, especially local photographers Attwood, End, Longhurst and Ree. I am deeply indebted to many people who have lent me their treasures – especially Percy Hathaway who came to my assistance at a vital moment. Grateful thanks also to E. Fenton, D. Johnson, Revd S. Jones, L. and C. Weightman, P. Kingsford of Windsor and the late Fred Bowyer. The Berkshire Libraries at Reading and the Durning Library have been invaluable, in particular the personal help of Mrs E. Moore who is in charge of the Durning Local History Archives. I extend my appreciation also to the Egham Historical Society, The Oliver Collection held at the R.H.C. as well as local churches and schools, all who have been most cooperative in my search for historical material. Finally it is impossible to conclude these tributes without putting on record my sincerest thanks to the immense support given by my family – especially my wife who has transcribed my disjointed notes into comprehensible typescript.

Contents

Foreword

The accepted pioneers of photography were a Frenchman, Louis Daguerre, and an Englishman, Henry Fox Talbot. The former who died in 1859 was the first to produce a high quality, fixed photographic image. The process was difficult and expensive to use but gave a very good image on a metal plate. The technique was quickly exploited and under the inventor's patent portrait studios opened in big cities all over the Western world. Fox Talbot, however, was the man who invented the more commercially useful process from which was derived modern photography. His innovation was the introduction of a paper negative which allowed the production of multiple prints and at a relatively low cost.

The internationally-famous cultural event of the nineteenth century was the Great Exhibition of 1851 held in the Crystal Palace; photographs of the event are extremely rare because Louis Daguerre and Henry Fox Talbot were about the only people experimenting with the camera at that time. By 1880 photography was the 'social miracle of the age' and most towns in Europe had at least one photographer to record people, places and events. By 1900 the first grainy moving pictures were being watched in awe. Few, if any, of the early pioneers of photography realised at the time they took their 'snaps' that a moment in time was being captured for generations unborn. By their efforts we are able to catch a brief glimpse of the people, events and scenery that have now become a very different past.

This compilation is not a history book in the traditional sense but might well be accepted as a busy person's guide to the development and character of the area around Ascot. Those of us fortunate enough to live hereabouts will fully understand the sentiments expressed by the late Duke of Windsor when he wrote: 'The Fort laid hold of me in many ways. Soon I came to love it as I loved no other material thing – perhaps because it was so much of my own creation. More and more it became for me a peaceful, almost enchanted anchorage, where I found refuge from the cares and turmoil of life'.

Introduction

Mention Ascot and many people will think of horses and horseracing, perhaps fashionably dressed ladies, but not much more. There is more to it than that. Its pleasant location amid rolling heath and the fresh air of East Berkshire, as well as its nearness to London, has for a long time tempted those able to afford it to build their large houses here and turn the surrounding estates into parkland. The proximity, too, of Windsor Great Forest was a considerable attraction. To support the operation of racecourse and provide services to the great houses, a local workforce was required and the population of the area expanded accordingly.

In due time the railway reached out from London and the district became ripe for development. The new arrivals lived in smaller villas and many of them travelled daily by train to and from the capital. This development slowly altered the nature of the place. Gradually, either to seek peace and quiet elsewhere or because of reduced means, many of the old wealthy moved away. Some former estates were broken up and houses demolished.

It was more or less at this stage that the photographer came upon the scene. The old pictures in this book, together with the accompanying text, offer a guided tour of the Ascot area as it once was, predominantly in the post-railway age. They will give the reader with a passing interest some indication of how things were and for the local inhabitant, reminders to stir the memory. Despite the relative scarcity of readily available material, the compiler has mustered over 200 illustrations. This book has been a labour of love requiring much detective work and tenacity.

Reg Morris has lived in Ascot for over twenty years and has come to know much of its history. A retired history teacher, for the last seventeen years he has been Chairman of the nearby Bracknell and District Historical Society. He has previously published *Distant Views from Sunninghill*; in the present book he focuses more closely on particular local scenes.

I leave you in his company. I think you will enjoy it.

Bernard Slatter.

President
Bracknell & District Historical Society

Ascot High Street, looking east, *c.* 1920.

Sunninghill Park Lodge, *c.* 1912.

One
Central Ascot

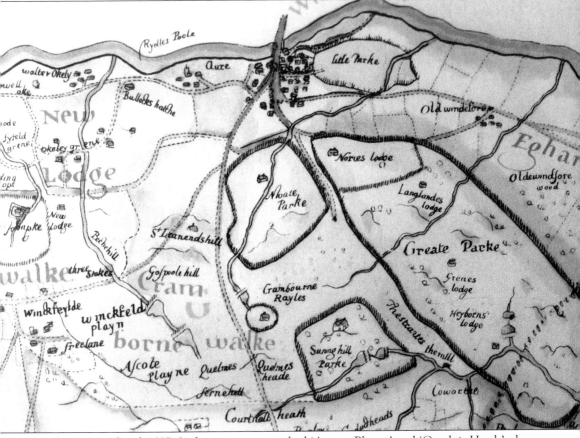

Norden's map, dated 1607. It shows an area marked 'Ascote Playne' and 'Conduit Heads', the latter with adjacent buildings, later known as the Wells. These chalybeate springs were identified as being of medicinal value and in time became part of the spa-water drinking fashion that was so popular by 1700. Bath, Leamington, Buxton and Tunbridge Wells were the most popular and famous but those at Sunninghill were considered to be quieter and more select. At this time, such maps could only be drawn as seen from the saddle of a horse and from accessible church towers. This accounts for some of the inaccuracies, although with balloon observation still one and a half centuries away, they served a very useful purpose.

Ascot Heath Races by Paul and Thomas Sandby, *c.* 1760. This is the first and only pictorial record of Ascot at that time. Paul, best remembered for his series 'Cries of London' was particularly skilful at painting people, and Thomas specialised in landscape work. They were both surveyors and along with General Wade and the Duke of Cumberland were responsible for many of the principal roads built in the Highlands of Scotland to control the Stuart uprisings. (Reproduced from a painting courtesy of the Royal Collection at Windsor).

This is an early-nineteenth century drawing of The Wells by Louisa Wale.

The Wells Inn on the London Road, as seen from Ascot, *c.* 1915.

View from the Wells garden (left) looking towards the racecourse (right, behind the post rails) Queen Anne, a very keen equestrian, provided a plate prize on 11 August 1711, a date traditionally given as the foundation of the Ascot races. Paul Sandby, the artist, painted a picture of Ascot Racecourse in around 1760, showing a small wooden building constructed to provide modest shelter for the Monarch and a few close friends. As the starting-point for the races was close to The Wells, it was quite natural that the organization of the races, including the registration of riders and horses, should be carried out there. In any case it was the only commercial building in the area. Later it boasted of having sat 200 people to breakfast on one occasion; it provided accommodation for those partaking 'the waters' and was also used for dances and assemblies.

Ascot Police Station

The Old Court House (above) was used as Ascot Police Station and is a short distance from The Wells. The station was built to provide a base for Ascot's modest police force and as a way of dealing quickly with problems arising at the racecourse. This building virtually marks the run in to Ascot High Street (below).

This staggered crossing features a wooden 'finger' signpost which points to Windsor and Winkfield (right) and St George's Lane (left). To the right of the horse and cart is the Windsor Road, on the corner of which stood The Grange: the road was variously called Library Road, Durning Road and Winkfield Road.

In 1883, The Grange (above) was the home of Sir John and Lady Diane Huddleston. It was the nearest large house and grounds adjoining the racecourse. All that remains now is a splendid cedar tree at the rear of the Silver Ring car park. There were other similar mansions built nearby but these have been demolished during the twentieth century. Such buildings were The Hermitage (now a shop parade), Holmwood Lodge (now housing the fire station), Westwyke (now a car park and public conveniences), Ascot Heath House (now the Police Station), and Heatherwood (now the local hospital). These buildings used to be positioned on the left-hand side of the picture showing Ascot's High Street (below). The white-banded twin brick pillars, bottom right, marked the entrance to The Grange; the pillars were demolished in 1998 to enlarge a garage forecourt.

The railway, arriving in 1856, severed the two communities of Ascot and South Ascot. To maintain essential contact the railway was bridged over 'Bog Lane' (above) as it was known. Bog Lane forked into upper and lower Bog Lane which eventually became known as St George's Lane and Wells Lane.

The Durning Library was situated in Winkfield Road and looked out onto The Grange. It was originally a china shop and post office. This building and its adjacent properties were presented to Sunninghill parish by Miss Jemina Durning Smith, founder of the Lambeth Free Library. The old post office was converted and the other properties funded the new library for Sunninghill and Ascot. This facility was open to adults during daylight hours and men only in the evenings. As well as lectures and classes in art, craftwork and cooking, games of chess, draughts and dominoes were available; there was also a smoking room complete with spittoons. At a later stage, ladies were admitted on Tuesday and Friday evenings.

Shepherd White's Corner. A short distance from the Durning Library, the Winkfield road actually crosses the racecourse. On race days the road is closed to allow free passage for horses and jockeys. The road then passes the edge of Sunninghill Park and arrives at the crossroads known as Shepherd White's Corner. The name derives from a well-known shepherd, whose 'Tin Hut' on wheels stood at this important but otherwise featureless junction. His 'four-legged mowers' kept the grass clipped and in good condition for the course. Since shepherd White's day the crossroads have been 'staggered' and a roundabout inserted, but the nostalgic name remains. It can be seen here that the signpost, which reads Ascot (left), Windsor (right), Winkfield (straight on), has been relocated between the taking of each photograph.

Cissbury (above) the home of Sir Edward Henry, *c.* 1910. In the early-nineteenth century, Sir Edward Henry's father worked for the East India Co. He had considerable difficulty authenticating claims such as for wages and pensions because of the large number of Chinese 'coolies' employed, most of whom were illiterate. He discovered that by taking a handprint he could obtain a positive identification. Sir Edward Henry pursued his father's discovery, and his research made him the foremost pioneer of the internationally accepted practice of fingerprinting. The blue plaque (below) on the wall of Cissbury, which faces the racecourse, commemorates his achievement. A similar tribute by the Fingerprint Society is on his grave in the churchyard of All Souls, South Ascot.

The Royal Ascot Hotel, built around 1860, is seen here from two different angles. The building was erected on Kennel allotment, marking the apex of the triangular racecourse. A 1902 reference says that in addition to the 'luxurious accommodation lit throughout by electric light' it also had 150 horse boxes with sleeping quarters overhead for the stable lads. The phone number for the hotel was Ascot 6.

Two more views of the Royal Ascot Hotel, opposite which stood a mansion called Heatherwood, which was described in the sale details of 1906 as having nineteen bed and dressing rooms, seven bathrooms, various other spacious rooms, complete with stabling for seven horses, a glasshouse, kitchen garden, piggeries and electric light house (generating plant). Ascot Hotel was demolished in the early 1920s to ease traffic problems, and Heatherwood became a hospital. The War Memorial was shifted in 1923 to its present site by the police station.

Englemere, Ascot.

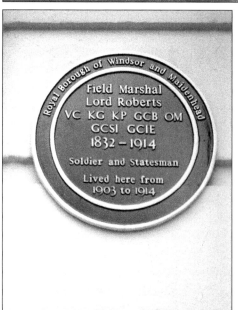

Royal Borough of Windsor and Maidenhead

Field Marshal
Lord Roberts
VC KG KP GCB OM
GCSI GCIE
1832 – 1914

Soldier and Statesman

Lived here from
1903 to 1914

Behind Heatherwood stands Englemere House (above). This was the home of Earl Roberts of Kandahar. Lord Roberts enjoyed a well-earned reputation in Edwardian times, due mostly to his popularity with the troops at his command. He was short in stature and wore a sweeping moustache as was fashionable at the time. A regular worshipper at All Saints church, he would have been buried there but his record and the nationwide affection for him decreed that he should be buried in Westminster Abbey when he died in 1914. This plaque (left) on the wall of Englemere House serves as a local tribute to his memory.

ASCOT CHURCH.

All Saints church was built in 1864 when the parish of Ascot and Winkfield was formed. The church was closely associated with Ascot Heath school in Fernbank Road, where in 1852 Mr and Mrs Sherlock were joint headteachers for the princely sum of £65 per annum. Field Marshal Roberts was churchwarden at All Saints; a fellow worshipper was Baron Huddleston, the last Baron of the exchequer, who resided with his family at The Grange. The gateway to the right of All Saints' entrance leads to the Royal Ascot Hotel.

Ascot High Street, looking east. These photographs, dating from the first half of the twentieth century, appear very similar but reflect the subtle changes that have occured over a period of almost half a century. The earlier picture (above) shows the High Street with a gravel surface pitted by cart ruts; there are only horse-drawn vehicles. The later images (below and opposite, top) show a 'tarmac' road surface and motor vehicles. This row of shops, which comprise Ascot High Street, developed from the original booths, sheds and crude wooden buildings which housed the blacksmith, saddlers, harness makers and corn chandlers whose services were required as the racecourse developed.

It should be noted that although the shop fronts in Ascot High Street have frequently changed, the upper parts of the buildings remain as they were originally, as seen in these two views. Most of the open-top double-decker buses at the time had solid rubber tyres over their cast spoked wheel (above, far left). The slatted seats upstairs had a sailcloth apron attached to the seat in front which could be unhooked and laid across a passenger's lap when it rained. Maximum speed, rarely attained, would be 20 miles per hour. The advertisement proclaiming 'Cigars 3d each' gives a clue to money value in the early 1920s. The banner joining the twin gatehouses (below) reads 'Benham House Yearlings' and marks the entrance to the Silver Ring.

This bus of 1930 vintage has just left the bus yard at the rear of the shops. Pneumatic tyres had, by this time, superseded the solid rubber tyres on cast wheels, providing a degree of comfort which was probably much appreciated by the passengers.

G.H. Butcher's print shop. In 1899, Mr G.H. Butcher (extreme right) came, for health reasons, from London and set up his printing business in what had been the old post office in Ascot High Street. His two grandsons have continued the family tradition, providing a quality service for over a century.

Ascot High Street, looking west. The dung-spattered road (below) shows that pollution did not first arrive with the motor car. Behind the cyclists there is a building with an arched faced gable- end and a small cross-like finial on the triangular apex. This is currently a post office and newsagents; its curiously ornate brickwork can be easily identified for orientation purposes. The buildings, from this building down to the shop-blind marked 'The Ascot Fish & Poultry Co.' and a little beyond, were removed around 1970 and a modern row was inserted.

The petrol station and shops shown here (above) in Ascot High Street were all replaced in the 1970s by a row of modern shops. Opposite (below left) is the current Esso petrol station, adjoining Hermitage Parade.

ACT.74.   HIGH STREET. ASCOT.

Ascot High Street, *c.* 1930. Opposite the car on the left is the sign board of the 'Stag', the oldest pub in Ascot. It originated from a refreshment booth and was nearer for the racegoers than The Wells.

Another view of Ascot High Street, this time in the 1940s.

These extracts from the old Garrison Theatre (now Sirls furniture store) programme will revive memories of the time when such films were new and not repeats of old classics. A lot of the seats in the cinema were brought from bombed-out London cinemas and were of an irregular length and size, making the gangways rather hazardous.

HIGH STREET, ASCOT.

On the left of this photograph (above) is the clearing made around 1950 for the Esso garage and a new parade of shops erected where once stood The Hermitage in its spacious grounds. At the far end of these shops was Sirls furniture depositary which served as the cinema and dance hall for troops during the Second World War. The old fire station was next to the last visible shop-blind, just right of centre. Following a serious fire at The Berystede, £500 was raised to provide a steam-operated fire engine, and Mr Kemsley, licensee of The Royal Ascot Hotel offered free accommodation for the vehicle. The station building (above) was opened by King Edward VII in 1902, as commemorated by the plaque shown below. It became a shop eighty years later when a new fire station was built in Station Road.

A.D   1902
THIS BUILDING WAS ERECTED
BY VOLUNTARY CONTRIBUTIONS
IN COMMEMORATION OF THE CORONATION
OF KING EDWARD VII.

Ascot Racecourse, *c*.1920. This view (above) shows wild heath on the edge of the racecourse where many of the car parks, tents and other amenities were situated. Acquainting the area was a brown-skinned figure wearing a feathered headdress, a multi-coloured skirt and bare feet; known throughout the racing world as 'Prince Monolulu' (real name McKay) he sold 'tips' to the more gullible racegoers. Other booths and sideshows were also available on 'the heath', such as this steam operated round-a-bout (below) with its glittering brass, garishly-painted animals and murals, accompanied by the unmistakable wheezy sound of the music.

Ascot Racecourse has seen every British monarch since Queen Anne. There is a plentiful supply of pictures of the racecourse, such as these of The Heath (above) and The Stands (below), but few of the locality. Ascot did not go through the stages of tram to trolleybus; its foundation and development has been centred on the horse. It might have been said of Ascot a century ago: 'what a lot of space taken up for so short a space of time'. There was the space then, but now there is hardly a day in the week without Ascot hosting some event or other. Internationally famous bloodstock sales, dog shows, auctions, conferences and exhibitions are all part of its extremely diverse but flourishing industry – the *'piece de resistance'* being Royal Ascot Week.

THE STANDS   ASCOT RACE COURSE   W.H.A. 5330

King George V and Queen Mary at Ascot in 1912 – arriving at the racecourse (above) and taking their places in the Royal Box (right). The traditional royal procession along the entire length of the course was made famous when George IV, flamboyantly attired and with liveried postilions, delighted the racegoers with such an impressive arrival. It can be justifiably said that from then on, Ascot began to acquire the international fame it is now accorded.

The Royal Enclosure, *c.* 1912. King George V and Queen Mary are seen here arriving in style, surrounded by a fine display of the fashions of the day.

The straw 'boater', as modelled by a few of these racegoers around 1912, replaced the bowler or trilby for the middle-class fashionable male. The 'toff' wore his 'topper' and, in comparison, working-class caps were for 'doffing'. Rare indeed was a hatless person seen anywhere at that time.

GOLDEN GATES, ASCOT.

The Golden Gates, *c.* 1909. Little is known of the origins of the Golden Gates except that they were installed in 1877. The gilded lions and crests, along with the gilt-topped spear-shaped railings gave rise to the name. This splendid Royal entrance near the starting gate was first used in 1878 by Edward VII when he was Prince of Wales.

The No. 3 Platoon, 'A' Company, 11th Berks Home Guard, 1944. The CO here was the manager of the Berystede (requisitioned by the Military). The other ranks all had important work to do by day, and their weekends and evenings were largely taken up with military training in case of invasion. It is important to remember that the reality of these men's lives was very different from the comic image portrayed on television by 'Dad's Army'. The expertise of such men was necessary to maintain the gas, water, electricity, rail and telephone services that were continually being destroyed or disrupted by enemy action.

Two
North Ascot

Ascot Place, Ascot.   W.H.A.906.

The area known as North Ascot quickly runs into the ancient parish of Winkfield and the town of Bracknell. Kennel Ride was where the Royal Buckhounds were kept, close to Shepherd White's Corner. Nearby is Ascot Place, as seen here with its extensive grounds, follies and what must be the finest 'grotto' in England. Having had various tenants it was later purchased by the Heinz family (of baked beans fame), who in turn lent it to Ronald Reagan, President of the United States of America and his wife Nancy for their stay in England at Mrs Thatcher's invitation. The house and estate have recently been purchased by Sheik Zayed Bin Sultan Al Nahyan – ruler of Abu Dhabi.

Brookside (above), so-named for obvious reasons; on the west bank were a few cottages, barns and a small shop. Mr Bishop and his wife took over the shop in 1870 and it became Brookside Stores', selling everything from coal to clothes. Mr Bishop spent a great deal of his time making deliveries by horse and cart to the wealthy properties in and around Winkfield and Ascot. The shop remained in the family for about a century. It has changed hands but still provides a valuable service to locals.

Kennel Ride was so-called because this area contained the Buckhound Kennels. The Royal pack was first introduced here by Queen Anne.

The old Roman Catholic Priory, from which Priory Road takes its name; it is currently used as retirement accommodation for the elderly. This impressive building, along with a similar collection in South Ascot, reflects something of the intense rivalry that existed between the Anglican and Roman Catholic branches of the Christian faith in the nineteenth century.

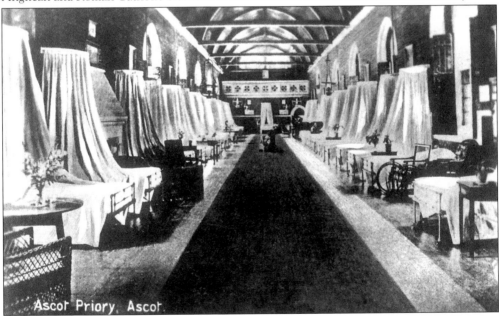

Heathfield was, at one time, the residence of Signor de Paravacini, an Italian diplomat. An extract from a score sheet of the Ascot Cricket Club (as reproduced on the next page) clearly shows how the Paravacinis almost defeated the Guards on their own. It is interesting to note that 'foreigners' playing for the local team is not solely a twentieth-century innovation. The match probably took place in the early 1890s, when the Cricket Club was founded and before Heathfield became a school in 1899. Adjoining Heathfield is what is left of Lily Hill House. The extensive grounds are now a rugby ground and public park. The house, recently occupied by Farranti the electrical engineers, is a sad reminder of glories past.

ASCOT CRICKET GROUND

The new ground on Ascot Heath was formally opened on July 4th by a match between the Ascot C.C.
and an eleven of the 2nd Life Guards. The weather was beautiful and warm and the spectators were numerous.
The Life Guard's Band was in attendance and added to the attractions of the day. The play resulted in a win for the home
team by one innings and 32 runs.

LIFE GUARDS

Mr French	c. Goodall	b. Freema	3	c. and b. P.J.Paravicini		0
Mr. Hughes	c. Freeman	b. P.J.de Paravicini	14	b. H. Freeman		2
Mr. W.Peel	c. Freeman	b. P.J.de Paravicini	6	c. Goodall	b. J.P.de Paravicini	9
Corporal Lindsay	c. Freeman	b. P.J.de Paravicini	0	c. Goodall	b. J.P.de Paravicini	10
Capt. Cunningham	c. Bruce	b. P.J.de Paravicini	5	c. Goodall	b. J.P.de Paravicini	0
Private Whitburn	c. Bruce	b. P.J.de Paravicini	16	c. Crutchley	b. Goodall	1
Corporal Pepler	b. Hawkes		3	st. H.de Paravicini	b. P.J.de Paravicini	1
Capt. Neele	c. Blackett	b. Freeman	1	not out		2
T.C.M. Robinson	not out		11	b. Goodall		1
Mr.Naylor-Leyland	run out		9	c. H.Paravicini	b. Goodall	1
Major Tennant	b. P.J.de Paravicini		0	b. Goodall		0
	Byes & c		8	Byes & c		4
	TOTAL		76			31

ASCOT

P.J.de Paravicini	c. Pepler	b. Robinson	2
B. Hawkes	c. Lindsay	b. Robinson	3
H.de Paravicini	c. Peel	b. Whitburn	95
H. Blackett	c. and	b. Robinson	2
F. Goodall	b. Robinson		2
P. Crutchley	c. Whitburn	b. Robinson	13
H. Freeman	run out		5
C. Hamilton	b. Robinson		1
G. Piget	c. Pepler	b. Robinson	0
W. Bruce	b. Whitburn		2
C.T. Murdoch	run out		4
	Byes & x		10
	TOTAL		139

An extract from a score sheet of the Ascot Cricket Club (see previous page).

The Royal Foresters Hotel (above) is a local landmark and is situated at the junction of Priory Road. It was here that the local hunt, as seen in the photograph below, would assemble to hunt in Swinley Wood, opposite the hotel. In the centre of Swinley Wood was Swinley Lodge, with an ice house, an avenue of trees culminating in a crescent, and sundry rhododendrons and brickwork providing evidence of an earlier building of considerable proportions. Two oak trees still bear the burned 'arrow' sign, used by special surveyors from the Admiralty to brand trees suitable for ships such as the *Victory*.

Adjoining Swinley Wood to the west was Martins Heron. It was a spacious building of little architectural note, 'standing in twenty-six acres of beautiful parkland'. The home, at one time, of General Charles Gordon (he of the riots and not Khartoum), it later became the residence of Sir James Scott, ex-Governor of New Zealand and Lord Lieutenant of Berkshire. When Sir James inherited his father's property at Rotherfield Park near Alton, the Sandemans (of Port fame) left West Mains in Ascot 'after nineteen happy years' and took up Martins Heron. The building was later divided into six apartments and finally demolished to become the small modern village, including a railway station and supermarket, which now bears its name.

Orchard Lea, like Martins Heron, is in the ancient parish of Winkfield. Orchard Lea was the home of Sir Reginald Baliol Brett, later the 1st Lord Esher. A nineteenth-century statesman with outstanding talents, his initials are to be seen in the terracotta insertion in the brickwork. He had two sons and two daughters; Sylvia, the younger daughter, became the Ranee of Sarawak (see ps. 60 and 69).

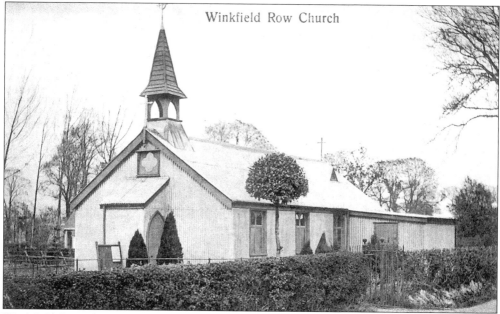

Winkfield Row church is a typical example of the 'Tin Tabernacles' which were built in the nineteenth century prior to the extensive rebuilding and restoration of churches that soon followed.

Opposite Orchard Lea is Winkfield Place, built in the first instance for a wealthy Windsor butcher who probably supplied the Castle with his goods. It has now been tastefully converted into five separate residences with a garden and lake. It is a rarity to find two such buildings so close together. An early view of the main building from the lake is shown below. The bell tower of the extensive stable and coach block can just be seen through the treetops (centre-left).

These two stacks (left) and various foundations (below) such as the one shown are all that is left of the famed Thomas Lawrence's Brickworks. With the advent of the railway in the mid-nineteenth century, the number of brickworks mushroomed now that this heavy product could be easily transported. Where suitable clay was to be found, several brickworks developed between Bracknell and Sunningdale. Lawrence's bricks were used for the Roman Catholic Cathedral in London, extensions to 10 Downing Street, and are seen at their best at the Royal Holloway College.

Three

South Ascot

From Central Ascot the road to the right is Station Road which terminated at the railway station. The area known as South Ascot lies the other side of the railway and until the railway bridge was built and the road extended, South Ascot, or 'the Bog' as it had been known, only had access to Ascot via Bog Lane. This basin of low-lying heathland had a reputation in early Victorian times for accommodating gypsies and providing the poor with a meagre living by peat-digging and casual work on race days.

Station Road. Ascot,

W.H.A. 1862.

The railway and its sidings (above, on the right behind the trees) were built in 1856. A doctor was required to attend to injuries and ill health sustained by the 'Navigators'. Since nobody could tell how frequently his services might be required, it was agreed that instead of payment, he would be given a large piece of land flanking Station Road. Upon this handsome 'pay packet' stands Ascot Wood House (below) and its grounds that stretch half the length of Station Road and back towards the Hermitage.

To mark the occasion of Queen Victoria's Diamond Jubilee, subscriptions were sought from the area around Ascot which resulted in the building of the Royal Victoria Nurses Home, as seen in both these views. It was opened in 1889 by the Duchess of Albany. Dean Liddel and his wife were closely associated with the project (it was their daughter who inspired Lewis Carroll's 'Alice'). The Nurses Home served also as the Cottage Hospital.

All Souls Church can be seen here to the far right of the nurses Home. Sir Edward Clive Bagley, ex Indian Civil Service and his four daughters lived at The Wilderness at the top of Bog Hill. The daughters started a Sunday School for the poor children of the gypsies and itinerants who dwelt in the area around 1850. Several notables in the area contributed to the erection of All Souls Church, Consecrated in 1897. As well as being a place of Worship contains a number of interesting links with the past. The East window is a memorial to Captain Mark Bell V.C. killed in 1916. The Bell family lived near Sunningdale at Earlywood Lodge. The Reredos is in memory of local resident F.A. Keating – of flea powder fame, and among others in the churchyard lies Sir Edward Henry pioneer of fingerprinting, also Sylvia, Ranee of Sarawak. The church was to have had a steeple but economy and stability deemed it remains looking somewhat decapitated.

St Mary's Convent. A little south of All Souls church is the Convent of St Mary's, built in 1885 in an area of thirty acres (given by Mr Devenish Walshe who was a local resident and benefactor) along with the Marist Convent and Heatherfield. It is rare to find three prestigious schools for girls in such a small area. The sudden growth of Roman Catholic and Anglican churches in the last quarter of the nineteenth century is an interesting architectural comment on the intense rivalry that existed between the two principal branches of the Christian faith. The Catholic Emancipation Act and later the compulsory Education Act gave a great impetus to church schools.

This view of the gradually developing village of South Ascot was taken from a vantage point known by the locals as Crown Hill. On the left is now the recreation field and the allotments were extreme right. The van (centre of photograph) is about to enter the High Street. The corrugated iron building (centre-right) was St Saviours, the first Anglican church in South Ascot.

This delightful statue of St Francis was presented to the junior school of the same name by Mrs (Bob) Hope when she was staying nearby with Mrs (Bing) Crosby. Bing and Bob were engaged elsewhere during the stay, possibly in Sunningdale.

The Council dustman and his cart near Cromwell Road was a regular weekly visitor. Many cottages just had an ash pit into which was deposited not only the ashes from the coal fires but all other domestic refuse. This would be shovelled into a basket and tipped into the cart. All too often the basket had to be carried through the house with an attendant trail of ash that trickled through.

On the eastern side of South Ascot was Bog Lane. The lane enters from South Ascot, under the original brick-built railway bridge and continues uphill (Bog Hill, as seen above) to Ascot. About halfway along, it splits into two parts, originally known as Upper Bog Lane (St Georges Lane) and Lower Bog Lane (Wells Lane).

View from Bog Hill, *c*. 1904. From the top of Bog Lane can be seen the area known as South Ascot. Photographs of this area give an idea of what the whole district looked like in Edwardian times in the last decade of the frail Queen Victoria and the nine years that Edward VII was King.

Two views from the foot of Bog Hill, *c.* 1912. It can be noted from the photograph (above) that the railway is up on a high embankment and is made from the very deep cutting through Sunninghill, reflecting that the railway is at ground level at Sunningdale railway crossing barely two miles away. The embankment was constructed at a time when pick, shovel and wheelbarrow were the basic tools, with the occasional assistance of a horse or two. The arch under the brick-built railway bridge was, until around 1920, the only connection between South Ascot and Central Ascot. The iron railway bridge that connects Station Road to South Ascot is supported on massive iron pillars and appropriate foundations due to the boggy state of the ground.

Brockenhurst Rd. S. Ascot

Two views of Brockenhurst Road looking towards South Ascot village centre and the railway station. A good deal of the boggy land has been filled in and built on during the last century.

Travelling along Berystede Road through South Ascot one arrives at the Cross Roads. The signpost points to Sunninghill (to the right) and Bagshot (to the left). Beyond the horse and cart is Brockenhurst Road and South Ascot; the section in the foreground leads to Sunningdale. Behind the signpost is The Berystede, with Greyfriars opposite.

The Berystede Hotel was once the home of the Standish family who hosted George V and Queen Mary for the races. The house was severely damaged by fire in 1886; the part shown here survived and is part of the original building. Across the road from here is Greyfriars and its pine forest, the English home of the last white Rajah.

Greyfriars is where Lady Margaret Brooke, the 1st Ranee of Sarawak lived. She was a well-known figure in Sunninghill, especially for her generosity to locals regarding her private cinema. She befriended W.H. Hudson, a notable Naturalist and accomplished author whose obituary in *The Times* pronounced him 'unsurpassed as an English writer on nature'. Some of his work was about and written on the Ranee's sixty acre pinewood at Greyfriars. The Ranee formed the Greyfriars Ladies Orchestra (below) which performed at the various house parties which were an essential part of the social round. By this means, Sylvia Brett and her sister Dorothy of Orchard Lea met Vyner Brooke, Sylvia's future husband. In time, Sylvia and Vyner became the second Rajah and Ranee of Sarawak with their English inheritance at Greyfriars.

Four
Sunninghill

From the crossroads at The Berystede Hotel runs the road generally referred to as Sunninghill High Street. These views show the street looking east (above) and west (below). The scenes, on closer inspection, give an indication of the undulations along the Sunninghill crest.

The main road in Sunninghill is about a mile long and changes its name three times. Starting opposite the Berystede as the Bagshot Road, it becomes Sunninghill High Street (as shown here), and then from the Cordes Hall onwards it is named Sunninghill Road. To the left of the parked cars (above) is the parapet of the railway bridge which crosses the line sixty feet below. The parapet is a tribute to the 'Navvies' who picked and shovelled their way through the sandy hill; the spoil was used to create the causeway across the Bog.

The cyclist (above) is riding along Sunninghill High Street and is about to turn into Queens Road where the shop window blind shields Edwin Belcher's drapery, clothing and book shop. This and several other photographs of this area were produced by Mr F. Ree, the village photographer, whose main work was to record weddings and family portraits. His daughter, Christine, played the piano for the school near their shop; she was also, on many occasions, invited by the Ranee of Sarawak to her cinema to play appropriate music for the silent films.

The Schools, Sunninghill.

St Michael's school was an 'all age' school. It catered for local children between the ages of five and twelve until 1914, when the school-leaving age was raised to fourteen years. The swimming pool at the rear of the school became the local Rifle Range after the First World War. Mr Morton, the blacksmith's son, was the village telegraphist; he was based in the shop by the school, which was then Sunninghill Post Office. To the left of the school is currently Sunninghill library. It was originally the cooking centre for the school by day. On some evenings it was used as a reading room for adults with reading problems, a similar service to that once provided by Durning library. To the right of the school is the cinema and Cordes Hall.

These young pupils of St Michael's school in the 1930s were not as crowded as they would have been in most inner city classrooms. For these very senior citizens of today there were no school dinners; two hours were given for lunch to enable many pupils to walk a mile or two to get home. About 5 per cent went on to secondary education; the great majority left school aged fourteen. These hopeful eyes had never seen television, jet aeroplanes, ballpoint pens or manmade fibres; even chips were still only available with fish.

To the rear of the local lads seen here, watching Mr Ree at work with his camera, is The Terrace containing the Mission Hall. Apart from the religious observations, the hall was used for music recitals for the gentry which were organized by the Ranee of Sarawak. On other occasions, villagers enjoyed listening to the pop stars of their time: Albert Whelan sang *My Old Dutch*, and 'Count' John McCormack's rendition of *Rose of Tralee* delighted the more romantically-inclined some years later. In pre-radio days such singers could travel the country with these songs and an encore without having to change their repertoire! Their efforts would be repeated less tunefully in the nearby Dog & Partridge in Village Road. Between The Terrace and the pub stood the Workhouse, complete with large kitchen-garden for those unable to afford the leisure-time activities which the Mission Hall and the Dog & Partridge provided.

The Terrace. All eleven of these cottages were up for sale in the early part of the twentieth century. The auctioneer's notice gives the names of the tenants and their rents varying from 4s to 5s 6d per week, bringing in a grand total of £136 10s per annum and described as a 'very sound investment'.

Sunninghill Ladies cricket team, *c.* 1908.

Village Road, Sunninghill.

Two views of Village Road, *c.* 1926. On the left at the far end of Upper Village Road (below) was the area occupied by the Workhouse and its kitchen garden. Able-bodied destitute men worked in the garden producing food for the inmates, and women did the laundry and similar chores, thus making this social service almost self-sufficient.

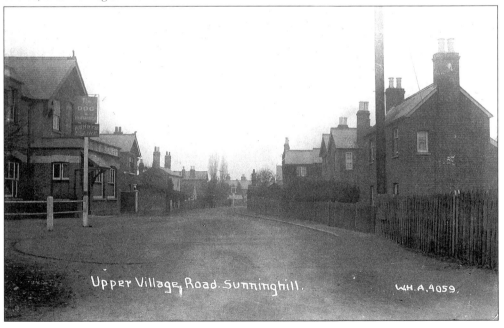

Upper Village, Road. Sunninghill.

W.H.A.4059.

The Picture House was specially built around 1920 by the Ranee of Sarawak. The Ranee and her son Harry used to invite friends to see private showings of films from London. It is said that the first talking film , Al Jolson's *The Singing Fool* was both seen and heard here for the first time outside London. It was usually the night after the Ranee had entertained her friends that local people were allowed in to view the film. In later years it became a public cinema; it is now the Novello Theatre, specializing in theatricals for children. The Theatre Company was based for twenty years in Ivor Novello's previous house Red Roofs in Maidenhead. Their first production at Sunninghill was *Alice in Wonderland* in 1989.

The Cordes Hall was pioneered as a village hall by Thomas Cordes, who lived at Silwood. He was the last Lord of the Manor and when he died his wife and family decided to complete the project as a memorial to his name and it was officially opened in 1902.

A gala performance at the Cordes Hall in 1908.

Opposite the Cordes Hall and adjoining the school was the blacksmith's forge, carpenters and wheelwrights. The photograph shows Mr Morton's employees – Mr Cooper the blacksmith (left) and Mr Duncan his assistant. In time, many craftsmen such as these became redundant. Mr F. Burke the undertaker, experiencing no change in his trade, took over the corner building. This area is now a small enclave of maisonettes.

Mr Morton, the Sunninghill blacksmith with his family, 1906. The son in the back row on the right went on to become the local post office telegraphist. Mr Morton became affluent enough to have a second 'smithy' which was situated near the Canon Crossroads.

The Cordes Hall, *c.* 1910. On the extreme right is the site of the Ranee's cinema, not yet built at this time.

The Bungalow, Sunninghill.

The Bungalow (above) is now Halfpenny's Garage and the entrance to Kings Road. The corner of the bungalow is just showing in the photograph below (bottom right); the shops (left) took the place of Morton's yard. Here at the junction of King's Road, the High Street and Sunninghill Road was the old Forge. To the right of the children playing is the Kingswick Estate and King's Road. This estate extended down King's Road until it met the access to Frognal (now the Marist Convent).

The last part of the mile-long road through Sunninghill, once a trackway to the church, passes the Three Jays pub and terminates with a roundabout. The old turnpike road cut across the track and severed the church from the village.

Kingswick Drive, built on the old Kingswick House estate.

CROSS ROADS, SUNNINGHILL.

The Kingswick Estate occupied the whole corner shown here(above). It was owned by the eighteenth-century Hon. Richard Fitzpatrick who was described as 'a *bon vivant* and gambler'. For forty years he was a close friend of Charles James Fox, Foreign Secretary (1802-06); both men came from long-established political families. The house was demolished and sold off, complete with effects, to pay off his gambling debts. During the demolition a complete porch belonging to St Michael's church was found forming an entrance to Kingswick's kitchen garden. The porch has been restored to its original place at St Michael's church and is celebrated by this plaque (right).

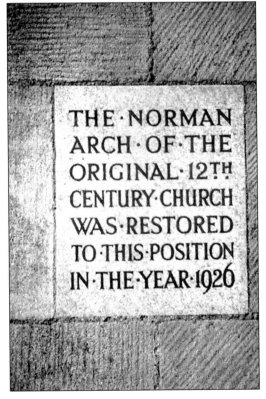

THE·NORMAN ARCH·OF·THE ORIGINAL·12TH CENTURY·CHURCH WAS·RESTORED TO·THIS·POSITION IN·THE·YEAR·1926

Kings Road, Sunninghill.

King's Road now connects Sunninghill with Sunningdale. A section of it known as The Rise, so-defined by the locals because whichever way you travelled you were obliged to climb a hill on the summit of which stands Lynwood and Heatherlands. To the right of the motor cyclist (above) is now the Ascot Post Office and in the foreground is the present entrance to The Marist Convent. Opposite the convent entrancestood the stately pile known as Pembroke Lodge; King's Road was a private road giving access only to Frognal (now the Marist Convent) and Pembroke Lodge.

Kings Road, Sunninghill

The 'Rosary' Marist Convent, known originally as Frognal. A covered way existed between Frognal and its next door neighbour Kingswick so that the families and guests of either place could assemble in the music room. The room was in a specially built separate building used for the social evenings and gatherings which filled the leisure time in those pre-film, radio and television times. The beautiful garden in the centre-foreground remains along with the original house (top right). The kitchen garden and the orchards (top left) are now classrooms for the convent school.

The original owner of Lynwood was John Hargreaves who also owned a good deal of the Sunninghill area. In 1864, he sold twenty-two acres to Sir Frederick William Grey, Admiral RN; his monogram is shown above the main entrance and cast in the hopper heads of the rainwater downpipes. The land was purchased for £2,500 and Admiral Grey built the mansion for a further £3,000. His father was Prime Minister (1830-34) and had a special mixture of tea made by Twinings to suit his palate: this gained in popularity and became the famous blend 'Earl Grey'. In 1878, the property was purchased by the Rt. Hon. Francis Wheler, Viscount Hood RN, a descendant of Admiral Hood of naval fame. In 1948, it was sold to the Motor and Cycle Trades Benevolent Fund. Lynwood has had several extensions built over the years and continues to flourish, both in occupation and reputation.

Heatherlands (above and below-left) is on Larch Avenue, which is opposite Lynwood and is one of the oldest roads in Sunninghill. It leads to Silwood Road and the Crossways at Canon Corner, continuing the old route to Windsor. To the right of the view shown below is currently the Civil Service Staff College.

This corner of Larch Avenue (above) marks the top of The Rise (below). It is a local name which has persisted, presumably because whether travelling from 'hill' or 'dale' one has a substantial uphill slope to contend with.

Five

Sunningdale

Sunningdale Park. This site has been occupied since the eighteeenth century and during that time it has passed through several hands. In 1930, the building was demolished and this present impressive residence was constructed for the new owner Sir Hugo Cunliffe-Owen. Sir Hugo was president of the British American Tobacco Co. and chairman of Cunliffe-Owen Aircraft Ltd. When he died in 1947, the Mansion and its sixty-three acres of magnificent parkland was sold to the Crown and subsequently became the Civil Service Staff College.

The Rise (seen here in both views) links 'hill' and 'dale' and continues to the Great West Road (A30) via Broomhall. Running parallel is Charters Road and both these roads are connected by Dry Arch Road. This particular part of Sunningdale has many large family houses standing detached in their own generous garden but, unlike Sunningdale Park, they are not on the same scale and are mostly early-twentieth century. Beyond Burge's shop (below) are several Victorian cottages to the rear of which lived Mr F.C. Hodder, a local historian.

Dry Arch Road (above) leads into Charters Road, where Agatha Christie resided in a house called Styles. Close by is St Bruno (right) the home of Prince Victor of Hohenloe. Both he and his sister were artists of considerable merit. Prince Victor sculpted the statue of his aunt Queen Victoria which is displayed in the northern quadrangle of the Royal Holloway College. The southern quadrangle of the college also contains the sculpting of Thomas and Jane Holloway. His best-known work is that of King Alfred in the market place of Wantage.

Two views of Charters Road. Agatha Christie's house Styles is behind the trees to the right of the man and his barrow (above) standing on the road. The main Staines-Bagshot road (A30) is at the far end of this road. A considerable amount of sand and gravel has been extracted from this area for the construction of military roads to assist with the manoeuvres which have been taking place in the area for two and a half centuries. To the right of Charters Road on the A30 is Braids, which belonged to the Twinings of tea fame. The family would have met Earl Grey at Lynwood during the frequent social rounds of Victorian times.

Charters: this very modern-looking building, set in extensive grounds was especially built in around 1930 for Montague Burton. He was a household name for tailoring in the 20s and 30s as the '50 shilling tailors'. His business was known for producing a well-cut jacket, waistcoat and trousers to measure for £2.50 current money! The internal layout and décor of Charters is very lavish; it is now the H.Q. of De Beers International Diamond Co.

BIRDS EYE VIEW, RIDGEMOUNT, SUNNINGDALE.   11657   PACKER'S
PHOTO SERIES.

Much of this area of Ridgemount belongs to St John's College, Cambridge. Due to the wandering vague boundaries, a dispute arose between the two parishes of Sunninghill and Egham regarding which parish Broomhall was in. After a protracted legal battle, Egham's claim was rejected and Sunninghill Parish recorded that 'Bells were rung in April 1735 for two days to celebrate the outcome of *Ye Tryall'*.

The official seal of the Broomhall Nunnery on a fifteenth-century document received by Chertsey Abbey.

Sunningdale Station and Hotel, c. 1910. Built beside the railway station (above, left) with its adjoining coal yards, sidings to the gasworks, and timber yard, is now a large supermarket and supporting car park. The railway is at ground level, as shown by the level crossing; it is some 60 feet below Sunninghill High Street, and 30 feet above the Bog at South Ascot. Most railway stations at this time, about 1908, had an adjoining hotel such as the one shown here. If one was catching an early train or arriving late evening, overnight accommodation would be necessary. The taxi service on show would have only operated during daylight hours. Mr Halfpenny advertised a 'Fly' for hire from his stables by the station. The large garage in Sunninghill still trades under the family name.

What was once known as the Great Western Road (A30) runs through the Parade (shown here) in Sunningdale, parallel to the old Roman Road (known as the 'Devil's Highway') which ran from Staines to Silchester. The Roman Road continues through the grounds of Fort Belvedere, under the bridge by The Ruins, under part of the lake, and through Egham to Staines.

Sunningdale Railway Station, *c. 1920*. The London & S.W. Railway line should have followed the natural direct route from Virginia Water to Ascot. Owing to strong protests from influential local landowners the Railway Co. was obliged to loop the line via Longcross to Sunningdale and thence to Ascot. The boundaries of Sunningdale are extremely difficult to define due to the close association of 'hill' and 'dale'. However, as in other areas, each is classified in this book as it is generally known, regardless of its political, postal or parish definition. The origin of 'Sunninghilldale', as it was once called, began with gravel extraction for military roads across the heath. With the arrival of the railway in 1856 a series of horticultural nurseries, beginning with Waterers, became profitable by supplying the extensive gardens attached to the large family residences which were increasingly being built on the cheap heathland between 1880 and 1900. This in turn provided work for local people. In more recent years, as in other parts of the area, some of the larger properties have become private schools, nursing homes or company headquarters. Several buildings have been tastefully converted into flats and many have been demolished to make way for small housing estates.

Broomfield Hall. On the corner of the Chobham Road used to stand Broomfield Hall, as seen here. It was owned in 1869 by Capt. Joseph Dingwall who happened to remark, in a railway carriage, that he wanted to sell it. Thomas Holloway overheard the remark and before the train had reached its terminus had purchased the house and grounds for £20,000. He had most of the building pulled down and replaced it with 'a mansion suitable for a gentleman of fortune'. He later changed his mind completely and bought Tittenhurst instead. Only part of the original coach house and stables of Broomfield Hall still exist; the remainder was demolished in 1931 and built upon.

Broomhall (above). The Nunnery, attached to Chertsey Abbey, stood approximately on the site of the present Broomhall Farm. One of the earliest casualties of Henry VIII's suppressions in 1522, the Nunnery leased out land as far as Portnall (now Wentworth), kept bees in an apiary on Chobham Common and provided refreshment and aid to travellers on the major road to the West in those times. Following the suppression in 1522 most of its assets were used to endow the new College of St John at Cambridge. A substantial part of Sunningdale surrounding the station (below) is still leased out by the college.

Golf Links from Kings Hill, Sunningdale.

The Golf Links. Sunningdale has earned international fame in the sport of golf. To offset the male segregation a ladies' golf club was formed: their Clubhouse was Dormy House (below). Times have changed and the house is now a highly respected retirement home.

Dormy House. Sunningdale.

W.H.A. 1550.

SUNNINGDALE, CHURCH.

Holy Trinity church. The southern corner of Sunninghill, known as Sunningdale became a separate civil parish in 1895, although it had been an ecclesiastical parish since 1841. Holy Trinity was built on an old gravel pit, gravel extraction for nearby military roads being one of the principal causes for the village's foundation. The church underwent several alterations in the nineteenth century including a chancel added by the Revd W.C. Raffles, nephew of Sir Stamford Raffles of Singapore (a man of similar standing to Henry Brooke, the white Rajah of Sarawak). Raffles worked for the East India Co. and by a series of astute deals purchased the island of Singapore and made it one of the great commercial centres of the Far East. King Edward VII laid a foundation stone to one of the many alterations made to the church whilst staying nearby for the Ascot Races. He was an annual guest at such houses as Coworth, Titness, Harewood and Sunningdale Park. Inside the church is a splendid bas-relief marble tribute to Prince Victor of Hohenloe, sculpted by his sister which demonstrates a considerable family talent.

Holy Trinity church (above) and the Congregational church (below). Both these churches, built around the turn of the century, indicate the expansion of population that took place at that time. It must be remembered that such places, apart from their religious function, were the only places where people could meet, exchange gossip and to 'see and be seen' as well as being informed on both local and national matters. The Congregational church has now been converted to residences.

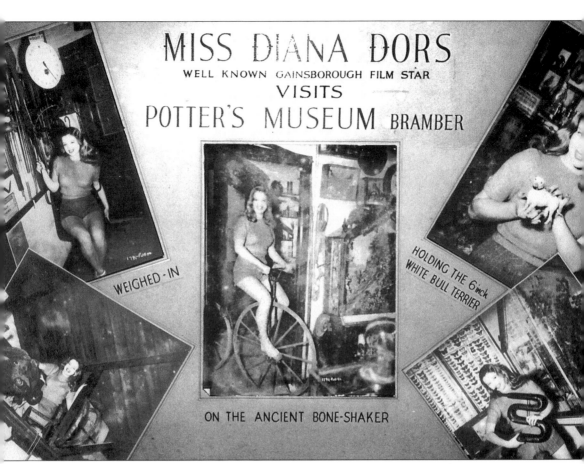

MISS DIANA DORS

WELL KNOWN GAINSBOROUGH FILM STAR

VISITS

POTTER'S MUSEUM BRAMBER

WEIGHED - IN

HOLDING THE 6 inch WHITE BULL TERRIER

ON THE ANCIENT BONE-SHAKER

Many celebrities from the entertainment world have settled in the area to seek privacy, peace and quiet. Diana Dors, the well-known twentieth-century actress, was a resident of Sunningdale for many years and is a well-remembered local figure. These exhibition photographs were purchased by the current owner of Jamaica Inn, Cornwall, along with the rest of Potters Museum in Bramber, providing an abundance of interesting items at the source of Daphne du Maurier's famous novel *Jamaica Inn*.

All hospitals before 1945 were maintained by grant and voluntary contributions. In addition to various fund-raising events, an annual carnival, such as the one shown here (above) on 22 July 1906, was organized in most towns and many villages. Scouts, Guides, Boys' Brigades and other youth organizations would combine with doctors and nurses to provide a spectacular parade of coal-carts, steam traction-engines and some motorised vehicles usually provided by the local builders. The parade was led by a local band; the group shown below in 1923 is the Ascot & Sunninghill Ex-Service Men & Comrades' Band. Playing in a local band was a social and leisure-time activity which was common in the south but traditionally plentiful in the north of England.

Ascot & Sunninghill Ex-Service Men & Comrades' Band, 1923.
Major H. CLAUDE HAY (President).

96

Gangs of workers, such as these men who were repairing the A30, were a common sight during the first three decades of the twentieth century. The horse-drawn tar vault was an open-top metal tank full of tar with a fire-box underneath to keep the contents fluid. This was laid over rammed stones to provide an asphalt surface.

Fort Belvedere. The triangular centrepiece of this building was built by Henry Flitcroft as a 'shelter-cum-viewpoint' for George III. It was enlarged, to form a residence during the reign of George IV, by Jeffrey Wyatt-Ville. In more recent times it became the residence of Edward, Prince of Wales: it was here that as King Edward VIII he signed the Deed of Abdication and went into exile as the Duke of Windsor along with Mrs Wallis Simpson, the Duchess who was the cause of his abdication. Some of the Virginia Water Ruins are in the extensive grounds of the fort.

Coworth Park Farm. Dating back to Saxon times when it was recorded as Coworth Farm, the present building has evolved as a half-timbered brick and *stucco* edifice. It is surmounted by a clock and bell cupola and is extremely pleasant to look at, especially as it is set in delightful surroundings. Its close neighbours are Fort Belvedere, Tittenhurst and Coworth Park (once the residence of Lord Derby). Strictly speaking, the Farm, Cowarth Park and Tittenhurst are in Sunninghill. As a point of interest, in the same year as Queen Anne's foundation of the racecourse, Edward Lane of Coworth died, aged ninety-eight. He had lived through the reigns of ten different sovereigns and a decade of republicanism; he was finally buried at St Michaels, Sunninghill.

Entrance gates to Tittenhurst, which was purchased by Thomas Holloway so that he would be nearby to oversee his projects at the Sanatorium and the College. In the twentieth century, Tittenhurst became the home of two of the Beatles, first John Lennon and later Ringo Starr. The building, although listed, bears little resemblance to the original and the sixty-two acres in which it stands is currently the English residence of Sheik Zahad, President of the United Arab Republics.

The Crossways, Sunninghill

The Crossways is variously known as 'the crossroads', 'Cannon Corner', or 'Silwood Crossways', and it marks the junction of the old trackway from Bagshot, via old Sunningdale to Windsor. It is along this road that Charles I was escorted as a prisoner to Windsor in the winter of 1648 and from thence to his execution in Whitehall, January 1649. The main road bisecting the crossroads was installed by the Windsor Turnpike Trust in 1759 and the triangular green is where the Toll House stood. The road to Windsor, to the left of the two photographs, cuts across the 'arc' of Cheapside, passes Sunninghill Park and proceeds through the Great Park into Sheet Street, Windsor.

The signpost at The Crossways points to Windsor (left) and Sunningdale (right). The foreground is the old Turnpike Road and the Toll House was on the triangular patch (right). The road to the right is Silwood Road with the pillared gateway into Sunningdale Park – now the Civil Service Staff College. This road marks an accepted division between Sunningdale and Sunninghill.

Six

Cheapside and the Eastside

The Holloway Sanatorium. This splendid edifice was the first joint product of Thomas Holloway and his architect William H. Crossland. It was modelled on the Cloth Hall at Ypres which was for 'the professional breadwinner whose income ceases absolutely when he is unable to work'. The sanatorium was opened in 1885 by King Edward VII when he was Prince of Wales. From Virginia Water Station opposite the sanatorium the road leads directly to the Wheatsheaf Hotel.

The Wheatsheaf Hotel was erected on the site of an earlier inn which suffered when the Virginia Water dam burst in 1768. It became the unofficial H.Q. when the lake was extended eastward and the present dam (Cascade) was constructed. Opposite the Wheatsheaf was a large area devoted to the coach houses and stables for the inn. This area is currently a petrol station; the Cascade or overflow is situated approximately where the car is in this photograph. The water from the dam passes under the road and into the River Bourne and finally into the Thames. Beyond the same car in this view is the main road to Ascot; the lake and the Fort Belvedere grounds are at the junction.

Another view, from a different angle, of the Wheatsheaf Hotel, to the left of which (through the trees) is the Wentworth Estate. The estate was once owned by Culling Charles Smith, Under Secretary of State in the Foreign Office, and his wife Lady Anne who was the sister of the Duke of Wellington. In 1854, it was purchased by Count Ramon Cabrera de Morella, with whom the Duke had shared military action in Spain. Marianne Cabrera lived until she was ninety and is buried along with the Count in Christchurch graveyard, Virginia Water. Ada Cabrera finally sold Wentworth as forty-six lots by auction; W.G. Tarrant, a by-fleet builder, purchased the majority of these lots. Some exclusive houses were built on the estate, one of which became the temporary home of the Duchess of York in recent times. The remainder became the internationally-famous golf course. The original Wentworth House is preserved as the clubhouse.

The Royal Holloway College, opened by Queen Victoria in 1886, and Prince Victor's sculptures of Queen Victoria (left) and Thomas and Jane Holloway (right).

Virginia Water Lake. The border between Berkshire and Surrey cuts across the lake by Fort Belvedere. The Berkshire portion was created by the Duke of Cumberland's soldiers after his fearful destruction of the Scots at Culloden in 1745. He dammed the River Virginia to form the lake but the dam was washed away in 1768. The Surrey portion was added when the present dam was constructed under the direction of George III. The lake had a small fleet comprising a Chinese Junk, Royal Barge, a model Frigate and some smaller craft: these were under the command of Lt Walsh R.N. and six subordinates. The Frigate was variously named *The Brig*, H.M.S. *Victoria* and H.M.S. *King Edward*. It was used as a bandstand which was 'dressed overall' on the Monarch's birthday and, on special occasions, was festooned with 'fairy lights' which were small coloured-glass jars containing a short candle known as a 'Prices night light'. The Fishing Temple at the lake was used by George IV and was later converted to a picnic shelter for Queen Victoria.

S AND LAKE. VIRGINIA WATER. JWM 6380.

The so-called 'Ruins' at Virginia Water were brought from Lepcis Magna near Tripoli; they are of a pre-Christian date and are well documented, except for the statuary which remains a mystery. There is a record of some statuary arriving from Lepcis Major along with the architectural material. It lay for six years in the forecourt of the British Museum before George IV could afford to have it collected and carried by barge up the Thames to the Bells of Ouzely. It was finally horse-drawn up Egham Hill to its present site (one column required eight horses to perform this prodigious feat). At a later date some statuary from the Wolsey chapel at Windsor Castle was added. Thus, George IV would have been able to drive along a section of the actual Roman Road, known as the Devil's Highway, and past this ancient collection of architecture and sculptures. According to archaeological research, G.E. Chamber's paper (published in 1953/54 by The Berkshire Archaeological Society) claims that the orignial statuary were actually removed and dumped in nearby shrubbery. Over a century later Ringo Starr applied to the Windsor & Maidenhead Borough Council for a grant to repair and restore some 'Roman statuary' in his sixty-two acre garden at Tittenhurst (a mere stone's throw away). The Council rightly rejected his application on the grounds that since his garden was not open to the public, no public money could be spent on the restoration. There currently appears to be no sign of the items in question, and so the mystery remains.

Royal Berkshire Hotel. On the opposite side from Fort Belvedere, on the main road to Ascot, is this hotel. It was built for the son of the Duke of Marlborough, whose mother Sarah Churchill was a frequent visitor. During its interesting history it became a private residence for Colonel Horlick of night-drink fame; it has also been a school for the partially- sighted and, most recently, a first-class hotel which is always solidly booked for Royal Ascot Week.

Shenstone House functioned for while as a hotel, to which was added a small petrol filling-station at the roadside. Both the hotel and filling station became dilapidated and have since been completely demolished. The site was developed in the 1980s by the construction of an attractive neo-Georgian small estate. A similar enclave was built opposite Shenstone, where 'The Boathouse', belonging to Frognal and its lake stood.

Beechgrove House occupies the north-west corner of Church Lane and was connected to The Glen by the Iron Bridge. At one time the house and its ten acres was the home of a Dr Baillie, physician to George III. It later became the residence of the Rt. Hon. Richard Fitzpatrick, Secretary for War (1782).

Silwood Park, granted in the first place as part of Sunninghill Manor in 1362. It was a long time before a building was constructed here. Of the several which were constructed over the centuries, the present Silwood Park House was begun in 1876; it was subsequently purchased by Thomas Cordes, a steelmaster from Newport, Monmouth. The estate of some 250 acres is now the property of Imperial College and includes some other properties including Oakleigh, Fairfield and Ashurst, standing adjacent to St Michaels' church.

Two views of Kingswick Corner where, in the time of Charles I, there used to stand Kingswick House. The building had been expanded considerably by the time it was inherited by Sir John Elwick, M.P. for Guildford in the mid-eighteenth century. He rarely used it and by 1769 it had become an assembly room – a socializing place for those visiting The Wells. When the house became rather dilapidated and put up for sale, it was purchased by the Rt.Hon. Richard Fitzpatrick, a relative of Charles James Fox, who lived opposite in Beechgrove House. Fitzpatrick had the house demolished and the land sold into plots. On one of these the local lawyer and historian G.M. Hughes built his own house and named it Kingswick. One of the original urns that stood on the gate pillars forms a centre piece in the public garden belonging to the Kingswick Estate of Council properties.

The Cedars, one of the oldest buildings in Sunninghill, has its entrance in Church Road, near to Beechcroft, Ashurst Lodge and The Vicarage. It became the home of the Rt. Hon. Earl of Yarborough in 1836 and has provided spacious accommodation and superb views across Silwood and Windsor parks for many years.

A model of Sunninghill church 'in its infancy'. The model was made by a Sunninghill parishioner during the last few years of the old edifice; it has been carefully preserved by the maker's descendants for several generations.

St Michaels & All Angels: Sunninghill Parish church has undergone many alterations since its foundation in 890 A.D. The old Saxon church was reconstructed in the reign of Henry I between 1120 and 1130 and is said to have been 'of dark ferruginous conglomerate stone'. King John gave the church by charter to the Broomhall Nunnery. The Parish Room and Green adjoining St Michaels was sold to the Earl of Yarborough, who lived at The Cedars. The money from the sale was used by the Revd Thistlewaite (who was Vicar for fifty-nine years!) to make major alterations to the church. In 1888, relatives of the Holloways added a new chancel to the south side; it was designed by W.H. Crossland (F.R.I.B.A.) who was the architect of the Royal Holloway College and the Sanatorium. Until 1861, music came from a barrel organ with a repertoire of eight hymns until Miss Hargreaves, daughter of a local landowner, installed a keyboard instrument and regularly played on it for the church services. The churchyard has a yew tree on the north side which is said to be over 1,000 years old. Many notables rest in peace here; they include Jane and Thomas Holloway, the late Rt. Hon. Gerald Richard Fitzpatrick of Beechgrove House whose tomb is a listed monument, Rear Admiral Sir Home Riggs Popham under whom Nelson served, and Augustus Schultz J.P. who was later an owner of The Cedars.

The Iron Bridge was a local landmark for many years. It was built to connect Beechgrove, which at one time housed one of George III's several physicians, and The Glen, owned by Lady Greville. The bridge's purpose was to facilitate social contact between the two families. The Glen is aptly named since it is a cleft carved out of the steep hillside. The concrete abutments of the bridge are still visible set into the roadside banks. This book was compiled next door at West Mains five feet below the Glen ground level. Bearing in mind also that Beechgrove ground level is in line with West Mains chimney tops, it is possible to see why a full frontal assault on Sunninghill was impossible for horse-drawn vehicles before the Turnpike road was constructed. Even then, as noted, laborious modifications have been necessary including a curiously-shaped roundabout which was recently built.

The Iron Bridge, late-nineteenth century. The tiring slope running under the bridge has obviously taken its toll here (right) where it can be seen that the horse has been forced to take a rest so that it can continue pulling its cart with renewed energy. The bridge was considered to be a hazard to traffic passing below and was removed by the Ascot Fire Brigade in 1948.

The Victory Field (Sunninghill War Memorial) flanks West Mains, which was the home of part of the Sandeman's Port family before they moved to the grander premises and twenty-six acre park at Martins Heron. The Field was acquired and developed after the First World War and an appropriate memorial plaque was affixed to the pavilion in 1995 to commemorate those who lived locally and lost their lives in both world wars. Air Commodore Christopher Mount DSO/DFC attended the simple but touching ceremony, along with several proud and bemedalled Veterans, Council members and local folk. The War Memorial has been well used and treasured by local people; in these photographs men (above) and women (below) can be seen participating in needle-threading races in a sports day which was held, in around 1919, on the Field. It was enlarged in 1977 to provide a delightful picnic area and named 'Tom Green's field' after a well-respected and diligent Councillor.

The Victory Field in 1912 when the local football team dressed up for a charity match in aid of the tragic loss of *The Titanic*.

The Victory Field in 1995. A small crowd has gathered for a memorial plaque ceremony.

Completing the circuit around Ascot, The Wells (above) faces one end of the Cheapside arc. Cheapside enabled heavily loaded horse-drawn vehicles to detour around the Sunninghill ridge and continue south again to near Coworth Park and Whitmore Lane. The long-established properties of Silwood, Titness, The Cedars and Tetworth Hall, along with their extensive parklands, prevented any large-scale development inside this arc. The Turnpike road and the increasing popularity of Ascot and its needs led to Sunninghill village developing on the western side leaving the church and Cheapside somewhat isolated by this separation.

The Golden Gates   Ascot.   W.H.A 5239.

The Lodge and Golden Gates are an impressive entrance to the racecourse. They are quite a feature and for many years were used by Royalty attending the races. More recently, for traffic and security reasons, the Royal party drives across the park from Windsor changing to horse-drawn landaus on the other side of the building shown, and then drive the last mile past the stands to the Royal enclosure. The Golden Gates mark the original starting point for the races and their close proximity to The Wells underlines their mutual relationship.

To the west of what is now known as Sunninghill Park (shown here) used to stand a manor house called Eastmore in Tudor Times. It was inherited by Henry VIII from his brother Arthur and the former signed his first document here as King. The building which replaced Eastmore – Sunninghill Park was a military H.Q. during the Second World War. Operation Market, the airborne invasion at Arnhem, was planned here. After the war, the house was to be refurbished as a home for the then Princess Elizabeth and the Duke of Edinburgh. Unfortunately it was destroyed by fire. Before a new site could be found for the newly married couple the Princess became Queen and the matter resolved itself. Sunninghill Park was later rebuilt in a Tudor style to accommodate the Queen's son Prince Andrew and Sarah Ferguson. The young prince went to school in Ascot and the Ferguson family lived at Loworth, opposite the Berystede. Sarah became headgirl at Hurst School, next door to Agatha Christie's home named Styles, and eventually the Duke and Duchess of York took up residence in Sunninghill Park.

Sunninghill Park is marked by a small lodge at the junction of aptly named Watersplash Lane which leads on to the now-enclosed Windsor Great Park and Cumberland Lodge (the latter named after the Duke of Cumberland, founder of Virginia Water Lake and chief Ranger of the Royal Forest). The same post had been held by Sarah Churchill, Duchess of Marlboro' when she was a close friend of Queen Anne. In accordance with the custom of the times, Sarah Spencer Churchill connived to get her granddaughter Diane married to the Prince of Wales. Nearly 200 years later one of her descendants named Diane did marry the Prince of Wales – the rest is very modern history.

Sunninghill Park across the water, *c.* 1940.

Two views of Cheapside. Directly behind the pedestrian cyclist (above) can be seen the Thatched Tavern. Close by is the old road to Windsor cutting the Cheapside arc. The Thatched Tavern is one of the area's oldest buildings; it was constructed in the sixteenth century and although it has experienced many alterations, it still manages to retain some of its ancient timber framework.

Harewood Lodge (above) and Titness Park (below). Some of the larger properties in this area have been demolished and family houses with good-sized gardens have been erected in their place. This seems to be a modern necessity which affects all the Home Counties, not just Berkshire.

Blacknest Tea Rooms, c. 1926. The pub on the extreme right, variously known as the Seven Stars, the Chukka, and Ascot Oriental, partially obscures another pub, variously named the Rising Sun and now the Belvedere. The signboard mounted on a single post by the bridge reads 'Rising Sun Hotel, Luncheons & Teas'. The white cottage also has a board saying 'Teas, Refreshments, Cycles Repaired' and the bungalow also has a sign (extreme right) advertising 'Teas'. For those arriving by charabanc in the 1920s these signs would have been most welcome. Both the cottage and the house are still extant on this sharp bend in the Virginia Water/Ascot main road (A329) with the Cheapside road at the base of the pub/restaurant currently named The Ascot Oriental.

Blacknest. Entrance to Windsor Great Park.

Blacknest Gate and Whitmore Lane terminated the Cheapside arc. It is worth noting that after the Civil War a large number of Cromwell's soldiers were in the vicinity and their pay was very much in arrears. One partial solution was to give them plots of land in lieu. Instances of this and what was known as encroachments or shifting fences ('acquiring' marginal parts of the forest edge, squatting and the suchlike) led to considerable confusion and legal wrangles. By the end of the eighteenth century it was resolved to clear up the mess. This is thought to be one of the reasons why several irregular-shaped plots exist around the now enclosed and emparked Windsor Great Park (1813) with its various access gates.

Two typically large houses in Cheapside: Buckhurst House (above) and Pemberton Lodge (below) complete with impressive gardens. Cheapside contained at least one mill powered by the River Virginia. It or they would have attracted those wishing to obtain its services and in turn would have led to some trading, hence the common name Cheapside – Anglo Saxon for trading post or small market place. This ancient part of Sunninghill remains sandwiched between the main road and Windsor Park and continues to retain its village charm, as evidenced by premises such as these.

Silwood Corner, late-nineteenth century. The twin pillars on the right give access to Sunningdale Park and the Civil Service Staff College. The caption printed on the postcard suggests that the gateway on the left led to Whitmore Lodge, a quarter of a mile further south.

'The Golden Gates' – Ascot

Bibliography

The History of Sunninghill & Windsor Great Park – G.M. Hughes
A Short History of Sunningdale – F.C. Hodder
History of Sunninghill – Searle
Chavey Up Down & Around – R. Timbrell
History of Orchard Lea – Clare Moore
The Ruins at Virginia Water – G.E. Chambers
Windsor Turnpike Trust – A.J. Heelas
The Secret Papers of the Duke of Windsor – M. Bloch
Extracts from the Past: Ascot – P. Smart
Royal Ascot – D. Laird
Cumberland Lodge – H. Hudson
Martins Heron:. A Family History – V. Hunt
Ascot News & Mr Toye's Cuttings – D.L. Archives.